Ball Games

THE MARSHALL CAVENDISH ILLUSTRATED GUIDE TO

GAMES CHILDREN PLAY AROUND THE WORLD

Ball Games

Ruth Oakley
Illustrated by Steve Lucas

Marshall Cavendish
New York · London · Toronto · Sydney

Library Edition 1989

© Marshall Cavendish Limited 1989
© DPM Services Limited 1989

Published by Marshall Cavendish Corporation
           147 West Merrick Road
           Freeport
           Long Island
           N.Y. 11520

Produced by DPM Services Limited
Designed by Graham Beehag

Library of Congress Cataloging-in-Publication Data

Oakley, Ruth
   Ball games/written by Ruth Oakley: Illustrated by Steve Lucas.
      p.   cm. — (Games children play).
   Includes index.
   Summary: Text and illustrations describe ball games throughout the world.
   ISBN 1-85435-077-3:
   1. Ball games—Juvenile literature. [1. Ball games. 2, Games.]
I. Lucas, Steve, [1]. II. Title. III. Series: Oakley, Ruth. Games children play
GV861.025 1989
796.3—dc19   88-28771
                                       CIP
                                       AC

ISBN 1-85435-076-5

Printed and bound in Italy by L.E.G.O. SpA, Vicenza

Contents

How It Began

Children throughout history and all around the world have had hours of fun playing games with balls. In 1492, Columbus found the natives of Haiti playing with balls made of a milky substance from trees. Children in Britain, however, did not have rubber bouncing balls to play with until the middle of the nineteenth century, when Sir Henry Wickham brought seed from the rubber trees of Brazil, which were grown at the Royal Botanical Gardens at Kew and the saplings transplanted in Malaya.

Roman children played with balls made of cloth.

Boys of the Gilbert Islands played with balls made of coconut leaves.

We know that Roman children had three main kinds of ball. For young children, there were large, brightly colored balls made of cloth and stuffed with soft material. Older children and men played games with inflated animal bladders very much like our footballs called "folles." Smaller balls made of sewn leather and called "pila" were stuffed with horsehair. A "paganica" was of medium size and stuffed with feathers. There may also have been solid wooden balls.

In Ireland over one hundred years ago, oval balls were made out of the cured skins of farm animals. Inside was a bladder, also from an animal, so that the "caid," or ball, could be inflated and would bounce.

Boys of the Gilbert Islands in the Pacific Ocean used coconut leaves woven together to make a large, soft ball. Children in kindergarten in Japan make **kamifufauen**-balloons made out of paper. Thin colored paper is cut into the shapes of flower petals and pasted together. Air is blown into a hole at the top to make the "kamifusen" a rounded shape. Sometimes bells are put inside.

English children make soft balls for kittens to play with out of yarn. They cut a circle out of thin cardboard and cut a smaller circle out of the center. The diameter of the large circle

must be about 3in. and the small one ¾in. Then they wind scraps of brightly colored yarn round and round the cardboard until the hole at the center is completely full. Then they carefully cut around the outside edge of the circle and tightly tie a piece of yarn several times around the middle of the hank. Tease the ends into shape and you will have a light, soft ball.

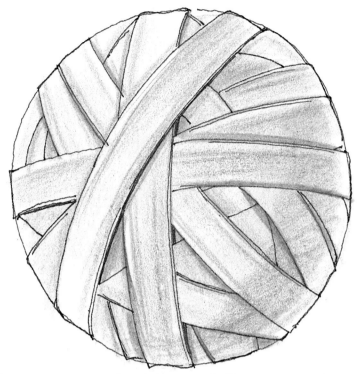

If you want a very hard, bouncy ball, you can make one by wrapping lots of rubber bands around each other. (Thick brown ones are best.)

There are lots of traditional rhymes with actions that you can play by yourself if you have a tennis ball or small rubber ball. Some of them need a wall to throw against.

If you practice, you will be able to play **Two Balls**. Begin with a ball in each hand, and throw the ball from your left hand at the wall. While it is traveling back, pass the ball in your right hand to your left so that you can catch the ball with your right. As you improve, you will be able to keep both balls moving all the time and do the actions for the games as well.

In Belfast, Northern Ireland, children chant:

> *I love coffee, I love tea,*
> *I love the boys and they love me.*
> *Tell your mother to shut her tongue*
> *That she had a boyfriend when she was young.*

As you get to the word at the end of each line, throw the ball over instead of under. The next rhyme has similar actions, but you have to pretend to eat cherries as well.

Two, four, six, eight,
Mary's at the cottage gate,
Eating cherries off a plate,
Two, four, six, eight.

As you get better, you could try this one.

Charlie Chaplin went to France
To teach the ladies how to dance:
This is the way he taught them:
Heel, toe, under you go!

(Point your heel and then your toe and throw the ball under your leg.)

Charlie Chaplin ran a mile,
He took a penny from a child,

(Pass the ball behind your back.)

When the child began to cry,

(Rub your eyes.)

Charlie Chaplin said good-bye.

(When you say "good-bye" turn around.)

You can imagine what the actions are to this rhyme for two balls. When you can get to the end without dropping a ball, you can consider yourself an expert!

When I was one, I sucked my thumb, sucked my thumb.
When I was two, I buckled my shoe, buckled my shoe.
When I was three, I banged my knee, banged my knee.
When I was four, I knocked at the door, knocked at the door.
When I was five, I sat on a hive, sat on a hive.
When I was six, I picked up sticks, picked up sticks.
When I was seven, I went to Devon, went to Devon.
When I was eight, I shut the gate, shut the gate.
When I was nine, I hung the washing on the line.
When I was ten, I started again and threw the ball right over.

A similar one is based on the Nursery Rhyme.

One two, buckle my shoe.
Three four, knock at the door.
Five six, pick up sticks.
Seven eight, open the gate.
Nine ten, my black hen.

This one will really test your skill!

I heard the King say
Quick march!
Under the arch!
Salute to the King!
Bow to the Queen!
Sit down, kneel down,
Touch the ground.

The traditional way to play **Ball Hopscotch** is to draw a simple rectangle on the sidewalk with chalk and divide it into five equal, numbered strips.

Each player has to bounce the ball in each of the strips, saying a rhyme without touching any of the lines or catching the ball.

One of the traditional rhymes is *Loopity Light*.

Here we go Loopity Loo,
Here we go Loopity Light,
Here we go Loopity Loo
All on a Saturday night.

Lift your left leg up,
Put your left leg down,
Shake it a little, a little
And turn yourself around.

Games to play with Friends

Queenie is a ball game to play with friends. "Queenie" has the ball and the rest of the players stand about four yards behind her, side by side in a line. "Queenie" throws the ball

backwards over her head. If anyone saves the ball before it falls, she becomes "Queenie." If not, then someone picks up the ball and hides it behind her back. "Queenie" then turns around and tries to guess who has the ball. If she guesses correctly, "Queenie" gets another turn; if not, the person who is holding the ball becomes the new "Queenie."

Piggy in the Middle is an easy game for three. Two of you stand about three yards apart with "Piggy" in between you. You throw the ball to each other, and "Piggy" tries to intercept it. If "Piggy" catches it, the one who threw the ball last becomes the new "Piggy."

There are many games in which a group of children stand in a ring and throw and catch a ball. Players who drop the ball are eliminated, so that eventually a winner is left. One version is **Donkey**. Anyone who drops the ball, has to call out a letter of the word "donkey" in turn. When "y" is reached, that person is out. The game carries on until there is a winner.

In a different version, a player who drops the ball must catch it with one hand next time. If he succeeds, he carries on as normal. If he fails, he has to catch the ball with one hand and stand on one leg. If he fails again, he has to kneel down. This is his last chance; if he drops it again, he will be out. The forfeits can be redeemed in turn, so if he gets to the stage of kneeling down, he has to catch the ball three times before he is allowed to catch with both hands. People who are out stay in the ring and the rest throw over them.

Windspel and **Trapball** are two old games which are very similar to each other. Windspel comes from the Scandinavian countries and Trapball from Britain. A piece of wood is balanced on a flat stone or brick. A ball is placed on one end of the piece of wood; then the other end of the wood is hit sharply with a stick, causing the ball to fly into the air. In Windspel, the player shouts "Windspel" and the name of the person whom he wants to try to catch the ball. If the ball is caught, the catcher becomes the hitter; if not, the hitter has another turn. For Trapball, the object was to hit the ball as far as possible with the stick as it was released from its "trap."

Games with balls and skittles, or "pins," are also very old and found in many countries. Bowling games were particularly popular among the German and Dutch people at least six centuries ago. When people from these countries emigrated to the United States, they introduced their games to their new homeland.

There are several ways to play these games. The most traditional seems to have been to set nine pins in a diamond shape and roll wooden balls at them from a line about eight yards away. In the simplest scoring system, each pin knocked down counts as one point. Men used to gamble on the outcome of these games and lose more than they could afford, so in the ninetenth century, "Ninepins" was banned by law in the United States. To get around this rule, people played "Ten-pins" instead and set up the ten pins in the shape of a triangle.

You can have fun with a set of skittles and a couple of balls. Arrange the skittles in a shape that you all agree on. This could be in a line, two circles, a diamond, or a triangle. Line up behind each other at an agreed distance from the skittles. The first person in the line throws the ball along the ground and scores one point for each skittle she knocks down. She runs forward and replaces the skittles and picks up the ball. While the second player has his turn, the first player gives her ball to the third in line and runs to the back of the line. This sequence continues until someone reaches the agreed winning score. If you do not have a set of skittles, plastic detergent bottles weighted with sand or a few pebbles can be used.

In French campgrounds when the weather is warm and sunny, children play a similar game with large plastic soft drink bottles filled with water.

Small skittles such as these are ideal for playing indoors.

Salazar's Obelisks is another game played with pins or pyramids and a ball or beanbag. This game originally came from Spain and Mexico. The pins are set up in two lines with a single pin on its own in front of the two lines. This "Queen-pin" scores more than the others if it is knocked down.

Hole Ball is a game from Russia in which a small ball is aimed at a series of holes. The game must therefore be played on soft ground, sand, or snow to make it possible to dig the holes, which should be positioned in a straight line, each about one yard away from the next.

The players stand behind each other about three yards away from the first hole. There must be as many holes as there are players, so that the first player in the line has hole number one, the second player has hole number two, etc.

The first player aims at a hole and throws the ball at it; if it lands in the fourth hole, he scores four and so on. The player whose hole the ball last landed in has the next turn. If the ball does not land in a hole, the last player chooses who should go next.

Decide at the beginning of the game what the winning score will be, and the winner is the first one to reach that score.

A game played in Belgium is **Le Furet**. Any number can play and all you need is a ball. All the players except "the searcher" sit down in front of a wall, with their hands behind their backs and their elbows touching the players on each side.

The searcher stands with her back to them and throws the ball over her head so that one of the players can catch it. The catcher then passes it behind her back along the line, hiding it from the searcher, who turns around and tries to find the ball and take it.

If the ball gets to either end of the line, it can be thrown over the searcher's head and she must try again. But, if the searcher finds "Le Furet" (The Object), then the person who was holding it becomes the new searcher.

Monday, Tuesday is a British ball game for seven players, each of whom take one of the days of the week as his or her name. "Sunday" begins the game by throwing a ball against a wall and calling out another day of the week, for example, "Thursday." The player who is "Thursday" has to run forward and try to catch the ball before it bounces. If "Thursday" succeeds, she becomes the new thrower, but if she fails,

then "Sunday" picks up the ball. He throws it at any of the other players and tries to hit one of them with it. If he does hit one of them, then "Sunday" has another turn; if he misses, it is "Monday's" turn to be the thrower.

The object of the game is not to be hit with the ball. If you are hit three times, you are out. If more than seven people want to play, you could use months of the year or colors.

Call Ball is a similar game which comes from Austria. Like Monday, Tuesday, it is played with one ball, a wall, and a group of children who each takes a name. Again, days or months are often used.

The game begins in the same way, but in this version, if the person called fails to catch the ball, she has to pick it up and shout "Stand" to all the others, who will have started to run away. She then throws the ball and tries to hit one of them. If she does, that player becomes the new thrower. If she misses,

she has to bend over with her hands against the wall, and each of the other players can throw the ball at her once. Then, the original "It" chooses a new thrower.

This can be quite a rough game, so choose a ball that is not too hard!

28

A game from New Zealand which tests the speed of your reactions is **Folding Arms.** Any number up to about twenty can play, and all you need is one ball, such as a tennis ball. All the players except one stand in a line next to each other with their arms folded. The remaining player stands in front of the line about four yards away with the ball.

The player with the ball may throw the ball to someone in

the line, or he may just pretend to. The player who is being thrown to has to make up his mind very quickly: if he is too slow at unfolding his arms and misses a ball that is thrown to him, he is out, but if he unfolds his arms and the thrower only pretends to throw the ball, he will be out for that. The winner of the round is the last player left in the line, who then becomes the next thrower.

Until about the middle of the twentieth century, boys usually wore caps whenever they went outdoors. Caps were frequently used as playthings as groups of boys walked to and from school, which was often a journey of several miles.

They did not only throw their caps around in games of catch. They also used to line them up in a row and throw either stones or balls at them. In Ireland, this game was called **Ball in the Decker** or **Pillar the Hat**.

Once one of the boys had managed to roll a ball into one of the lined-up caps, the owner of the cap would run up and take the ball out of the cap. He then threw it to try to hit one of the

This picture, taken in 1911, shows a group of boy coal miners. Notice that they are all wearing caps.

other boys with it. If he missed, a pebble was put in his cap, but if he hit a boy, a pebble was put in the cap of the boy he hit.

When a boy had a previously agreed number of pebbles in his hat, he had to stand up with his back to a wall and one arm outstretched, with his hand against the wall. Each of the other lads then had one turn to throw the ball and try to hit his hand.

A modern and less painful version of this game is **Pitch Ball.** It can be played indoors or out, and by any number and age of players. Set up a row of containers like wastebaskets or empty cartons or pots and pans. Mark a line with chalk, about two or three yards away from the targets. The players have to take turn to try and throw a ball to land in one of the objects. If you like, assign different scores to different targets, according to their size and difficulty. The winner is the first to reach an agreed score.

Team Games with a Ball

If you have a large grassy area and ten or more players, you could play **Bamboula,** a very old team game from the Caribbean. You need some equipment and preparation. Each player needs two rackets. You could use badminton rackets or ping pong bats with sticks tied to them to make long handles. You also need a small rubber ball. You also need two pieces of board or tin about two yards high to make the goals which are placed at each end of the field. The "bamboula" is a pole set up in the middle of the field.

To start the game, the ball is tossed up at the "bamboula," and the players use their two bats to scoop up the ball from the ground and to pass it so that they can score a goal by hitting the board at their end of the field.

The Indians of Mexico in the fifteenth century played a ball game called **Tlachtli.** It was played indoors on a long, narrow court with high walls, which had stones at the top with holes in them. The holes were the same size as the large ball with which the Indians played. They wore carved stone belts which had knobs on them which they used to knock the ball around the court by bending and twisting their hips. The aim of the game was to knock the ball into the holes in the stones. Sometimes, it was played very seriously as a ceremony, and the loser would be sacrificed to the gods.

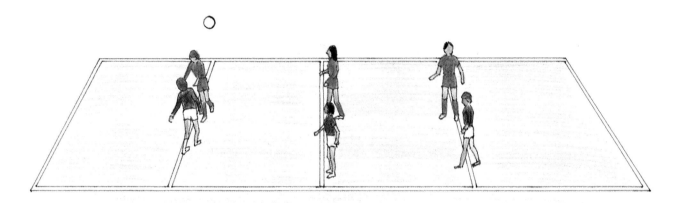

Today, children play a modern version of Tlachtli just for fun called **Bumpball.** Two teams are divided into an equal number of centers, middies and ends. You need a large, light ball and a space about the size of a basketball court. The court has to be divided into quarters with three parallel lines. The players stand on their appropriate lines, and the ball is thrown up on the center line to start the game. The ball is passed by bumping it with hips, backs, or shoulders. You are not allowed to throw, kick or pat it; in other words, no player can touch the ball with his hands or feet.

A middie scores three points for passing the ball to an end in his team, and an end scores two points when he gets the ball over his end line. Twenty-five points make a game.

Stoolball was brought to the United States from Europe and may be the origin of the English game of cricket. It is said to have first been played by milkmaids sitting on their three-legged milking stools which were called "crickets." In Tudor times, it seems to have been the custom to play for kisses, especially on May Day.

Nowadays, any stool or carton is used. The batsman stands in front of the stool and tries to prevent the rest of the players from hitting it with the ball. He may have a bat or stick, or he may just use his hands. The attackers stand about three or four yards away and take turns to throw the ball. The attacker who succeeds in hitting the stool becomes the batsman, as does any player who catches the ball when it is hit. The winner is the player or team who scores most hits before being out.

The game can be made more complicated (and more like cricket) by having another "wicket" (stool) and allowing the defender to run between the two to score runs. The defender can be tagged with the ball by the fielders while he is running between the wickets.

Another game which traveled to the United States from England is **Pass and Catch.** It has been played since the time when Queen Elizabeth I was a child. Today, it is often played as a party game. The players divide into equal teams and stand behind each other in a line. One player from each team stands about three yards in front of the rest of his or her team. Each team has a ball, which is thrown, at a given signal, to the first "catcher," the first player in his team's line. If the catcher catches it, he runs to take the place of the thrower, and the thrower runs to the back of his team's line. The first team to get back to the beginning with the first thrower at the front is the winner. If any catcher drops the ball, the thrower has to run and pick up the ball, go back to his place, and throw again.

Les Boules is the French version of bowls. It is taken very seriously in France, where most towns and villages have an area set aside for the townsmen to play the game. Children also enjoy a more lighthearted version of the game. It can be played individually or in teams of three or four. You need a set of "bowls," which are hard balls the size of a tennis ball, but not bouncy. You also need a smaller ball for a "jack," at which the "bowls" are thrown. One player begins the game by throwing the "jack" into the "alley." The idea of the game is for each player to throw or roll his "bowl" and hit the "jack." When each player has had a turn, the "bowl" nearest the "jack" wins a point, and the next player throws the "jack" to begin the next round.

A more energetic game from Germany is **Voelkerball.** To play this game, you need a large, bouncy ball which is not too hard, and three benches or several empty cartons with which to divide up a large space into four parts (as shown in the diagram.) You need either a large room or a big open space outside.

The players, which can be any number up to about thirty, are divided into two teams and stand in the positions illustrated. One of the players at the far end of the playing area begins the game by throwing the ball and trying to hit one of the opposing team with it. If one of the players is hit, she must join her teammate at the end of the playing area. If a player catches the ball, she is not out, and she can throw the ball to try to hit one of the players in the other team.

Once the ball is in play, anyone can throw it to try to hit a player from the other team. The winning team is the one to have the last player in the part of the playing area where she started.

Any even number of players of any age can play **Tiger's Ball** from Israel. The players divide into two teams and form two circles. Each circle has a ball, which is passed from one player to another across and around the circles. Inside each circle stands a player from the opposing team, who tries to intercept the ball as it is being passed. The first of these two players to catch the other team's ball wins a point for his team. When this happens, two new players take their places inside the circles. The team with the most points at the end of an agreed time wins the game.

Another game from Israel which is played at children's parties around the world is **Leg Relay.** You need about twenty players, the same number of chairs, and two balls. The chairs are arranged in two lines facing each other, about two yards apart. The players sit on them facing each other with their legs held straight out in front of them.

A ball is placed between the ankles of each of the players who are at the beginning of each line. The idea of the game is to pass the ball along the line and all the way back, using only the legs. If the ball is dropped, it has to go back to the begin-

ning and that team must start again. The winning team is the one that first passes the ball all the way along the line and back without dropping it.

Le Lettre Du Traitre comes from Belgium and is played outdoors, preferably in a wooded area with plenty of hiding places. Any number may play, but each person needs a tennis ball or one of a similar size.

Before the game begins, the secret letter has to be hidden by the "traitor," who leaves clues behind him such as pieces of paper which show where he has been. The two teams of players begin from opposite sides of the agreed playing area and try to find the letter. If a player spots an opponent, he can "kill" him by hitting him with his ball. If he does not miss, he scores a point for his team, and the opponent who has been "killed" is out of the game. The player who finds the letter gains five points for his team. The finding of the letter finishes the game, and the team with the most points wins.

When families moved to a new land, the children took their knowledge of their own games with them and introduced them to their new friends, so it is not surprising that games like **Forceball** are played in countries as far apart as Australia and Britain.

Like Leg Relay, this is a team game for about twenty to thirty players and can be played in a large indoor space, or outside. All you need is one large ball—a basketball is ideal.

The players form two equal teams and stand side by side, with their legs apart and each player's feet touching the feet of the children on each side of them. The teams need to face each other, about two or three yards apart, depending on the age and strength of the children. To start the game, the ball is rolled between the two teams. The players bend over and, with their hands only, try to bat the ball between the legs of the opposite team. No one is allowed to move her feet, and the ball may be held only for three seconds.

Agree beforehand how many points are needed to win the game; one point is scored for each time the ball goes through the legs of the other team. If possible, a chalk line drawn behind each team can be the mark the ball has to cross in order to score a point.

Children in Uganda play **Hurly Burly,** which is a fast game with about ten players in each team. You need a large outdoor space about fifty yards long and ten yards wide which you can mark with a center line in the middle and goal lines at each end.

To begin the game, the players stand where they like as long as it is in their side of the marked field. The referee bounces the ball, which needs to be a large one like a soccer ball, on the center line and the players run to get the ball. They are allowed to kick, catch, throw, carry or pass it. The other children try to touch the player who has the ball. If they succeed, the one carrying the ball must drop it. If she does not drop it, the referee awards a free throw from the position where the player was touched.

When a player gets the ball across the other team's goal line, she scores a point for her team. The winning team is the one with the most points at the end of the agreed time.

Many children's games are a simpler version of adult ones, and children from the Russian province of Georgia like to imitate the traditional game of **Tskhenburti,** which is a kind of polo played on horseback with a ball and long-handed rackets.

The children divide into two teams, about twelve on each side. Each team then divides into pairs, so that in each pair one child will be the rider and the other the horse. A piece of rope (a jump rope works well) is passed across the shoulders and under the armpits of the "horse" to make "reins." Sticks with blocks of wood nailed to the end are used as bats, and the ball must be small and not bouncy. Goal posts are made at each end of the agreed playing area by positioning two posts in the ground about two yards apart. A small mound of earth is made in the middle of the pitch as the starting position. The aim of the game is to hit the ball through the other team's goal.

Dodge Ball is played in many parts of the world. In Britain and the U.S., it is usually played as a team game, but in Sweden, a player tries to hit anyone else with the ball. When someone is hit with the ball, he has to sit down unless he caught the ball. If the ball rolls by him, he can pick it up; then he is allowed to stand up and play again. The winner is the last one left standing.

To play Dodge Ball as a team game, you need about thirty
players, a large space, and a large, soft ball. One team forms
a large circle, and the other team stands inside it. The children
making the circle throw the ball and try to hit those inside,
who are allowed to run around and try to dodge the ball. The
players forming the circle are allowed to go into the circle to
pick up the ball, but they must not throw it unless they are
back in their places. Players may pass the ball to each other
before aiming at someone in the circle. When a player in the
circle is hit, she has to stand outside the circle.

After an agreed time, the teams swap, and the number of
players who have been tagged is counted. The winning team
is the one with the least number of tagged players after the
agreed number of innings.

As you can see, children around the world have always used
their ingenuity to have fun with one of the simplest toys of all.
Now you can enjoy experimenting with their games and
adapting them to suit yourself and your friends.

Glossary

alley   A long, thin piece of land or part of a room for playing skittles or bowls.

century   One hundred, usually one hundred years. The twentieth century is counted from 1900 to 1999, so the year 2000 will be the first year of the twenty-first century.

ceremony   A special occasion with traditional actions and speeches. Often concerned with religion.

Chaplin, "Charlie"   Charles Chaplin was born of poor parents in London in 1889. He had a very hard, sad, early life, but found fame and fortune as a comic actor in early silent motion pictures. He retired to Switzerland, was made a Knight, and died on Christmas Day, 1977.

Columbus, Christopher   (1451-1506)   An Italian sailor who served the Spanish royal family as an explorer. He was the first European to sail to the American continent, although he did not realize what he had found. He thought he had discovered a new route to India.

jack   In bowling games, the small, white ball at which larger balls are aimed.

May Day   May 1 which was celebrated in medieval Europe as a Spring Festival with dancing around a Maypole. It is still celebrated as a holiday in some countries.

obelisk   A four-sided column with a pyramid shaped top. Obelisks in the ancient world were usually connected with the worship of the sun.

parallel   Lines which are parallel always remain the same distance apart. They will never meet.

Queen Elizabeth I   A famous queen of England. She was born in 1533 and ruled from 1588 to 1603.

Romans   The race of people originating in Rome who, in the first century, ruled most of Europe and parts of Africa and Asia around the Mediterranean Sea.

sapling   A young tree.

Tudor   The family name of the Kings and Queens of England beginning with Henry VII (1485) and ending with Elizabeth I (1603).

Index of Countries

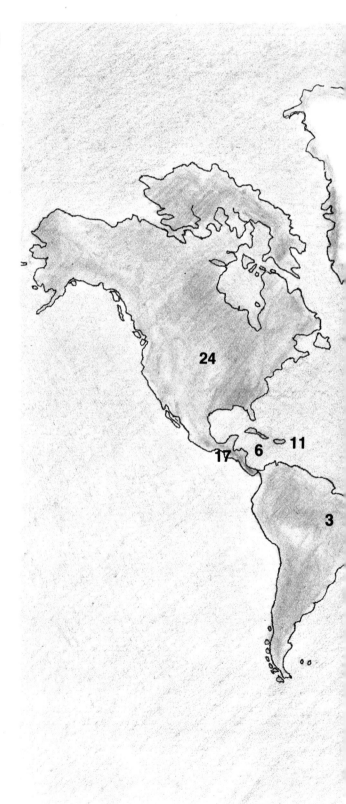

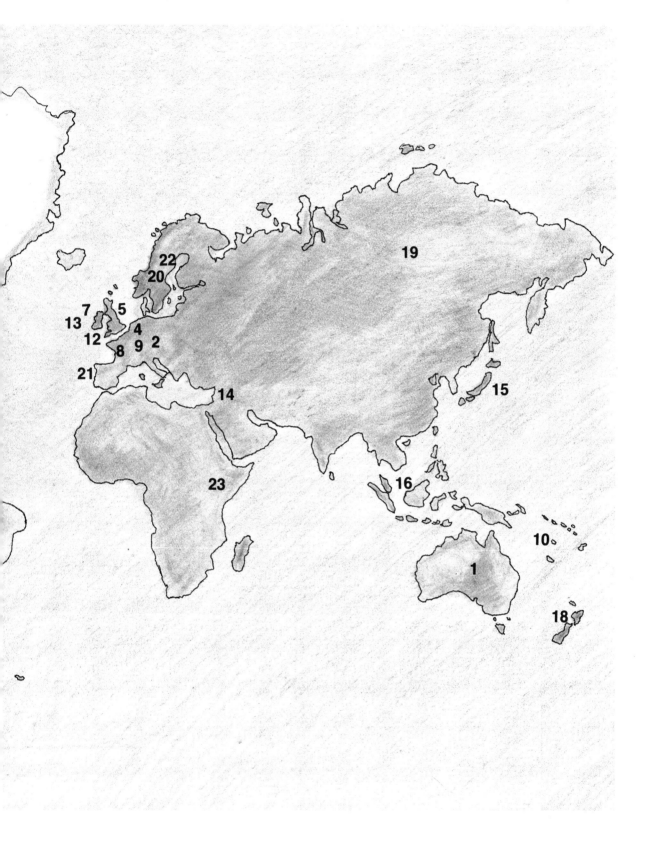

22
20
7
5
13
12
4
8 9 2
21
14
19
15
16
23
10
1
18

47

Index